GLOBAL GHOST STORIES

GHOSTS IN ASIA

BY MONIKA DAVIES

EPIC

BELLWETHER MEDIA • MINNEAPOLIS, MN

EPIC BOOKS are no ordinary books. They burst with intense action, high-speed heroics, and shadows of the unknown. Are you ready for an Epic adventure?

This edition first published in 2022 by Bellwether Media, Inc.

Library of Congress Cataloging-in-Publication Data

Names: Davies, Monika, author.
Title: Ghosts in Asia / Monika Davies.
Description: Minneapolis, MN : Bellwether Media, 2022. | Series: Epic: global ghost stories |
    Includes bibliographical references and index. | Audience: Ages 7-12 | Audience: Grades 4-6 |
    Summary: "Engaging images accompany information about ghost stories in Asia. The combination
    of high-interest subject matter and light text is intended for students in grades 2 through 7"--Provided
    by publisher
Identifiers: LCCN 2021011395 (print) | LCCN 2021011396 (ebook) | ISBN 9781644875377 (library binding)
    | ISBN 9781648344459 (ebook)
Subjects: LCSH: Ghosts--Asia--Juvenile literature.
Classification: LCC BF1472.A78 D38 2022 (print) | LCC BF1472.A78 (ebook) | DDC 133.1095--dc23
LC record available at https://lccn.loc.gov/2021011395
LC ebook record available at https://lccn.loc.gov/2021011396

Editor: Betsy Rathburn   Designer: Brittany McIntosh

Printed in the United States of America, North Mankato, MN.

TABLE OF CONTENTS

GHOSTS IN ASIA

Asia is Earth's largest **continent**. It is home to many **cultures**. Its history is thousands of years old!

MANY PEOPLE, MANY STORIES

There are 48 countries in Asia! More than half of the world's people live there.

Over time, creepy stories have developed. Many cannot be fully explained. Could Asia be home to ghosts?

THE BATHROOM GHOST

Japan is home to a creepy **urban legend**. Hanako-san is a ghostly schoolgirl. She wears a red dress. Her hair is cut short.

Some say she died in **World War II**. A bomb hit her school.

Japan

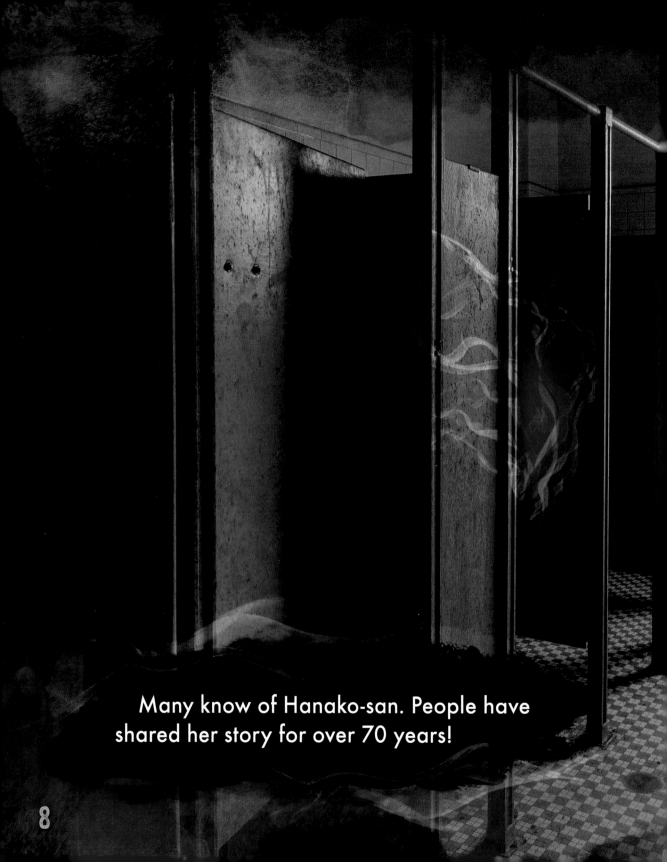

Many know of Hanako-san. People have shared her story for over 70 years!

KAIDAN

Japanese ghost stories are called *kaidan*. These are stories of scary ghosts from the past.

Stories say that her spirit haunts school bathrooms. She waits in the third stall.

Only the brave look for Hanako-san.
They knock three times on her stall door.

She might greet her visitor. She could reach out her ghostly hand. She may even pull visitors down the toilet!

THE ALEYA

Lights flicker in the **swamps** of West Bengal, India. Some think they are ghost lights. People call them the Aleya.

West Bengal
India

MANY GHOSTS

Many types of ghosts are said to roam West Bengal. Most ghosts are friendly. Some are headless. Others will beg for fish!

Stories say the lights are **stranded** spirits. They are ghosts of fishermen who died in the swamps.

Lost fishermen follow the Aleya through the dark. Sometimes, the lights lead them to safety. Other times, the lights lead to danger. Those who follow them often become lost. Soon, they drown in the swamp. Would you follow them?

IS IT TRUE?

People often see creepy balls of light in dark, swampy areas. The lights might be fireflies or glowing mushrooms. They may also be caused by gases.

THE LAST BUS
TO FRAGRANT HILLS

A story haunts people in Beijing, China.
In 1995, a bus was headed to a part of
the city called Fragrant Hills.

Beijing
China

But it crashed into a **reservoir** in the middle of the night. No one on board made it out alive.

Earlier in the evening, a rider reported a strange event before getting off the bus. She saw three men in long, **traditional** robes. A gust of wind blew up their robes. Underneath, the men had no legs!

19

Were the men ghostly **hitchhikers**? Did they cause the bus to crash? No one knows what really happened.

But many believe ghosts caused the accident. People avoid Fragrant Hills at night. What do you think?

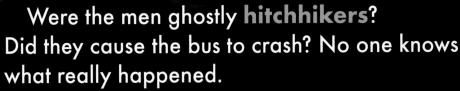

— CULTURAL CONNECTION —

Stories of hitchhiker ghosts are common. In England, a road called A229 is said to be haunted. A woman in a white dress asks drivers for rides. As they drive, she disappears!

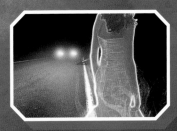

GLOSSARY

continent—one of the seven main land areas on Earth

cultures—beliefs, arts, and ways of life in places or societies

hitchhikers—people who get rides from strangers

reservoir—a human-made lake

stranded—left without the ability to go somewhere else

swamps—areas of low ground where water collects

traditional—related to customs, ideas, or beliefs handed down from one generation to the next

urban legend—a story that may be true or false and is spread by word-of-mouth from person to person

World War II—a conflict fought from 1939 to 1945 that involved many of the world's countries

TO LEARN MORE

AT THE LIBRARY

Andrus, Aubre. *Real-Life Ghost Stories: Spine-Tingling True Tales.* North Mankato, Minn.: Capstone Press, 2020.

Harvey, Jillian L. *Famous Ghost Stories of Asia.* North Mankato, Minn.: Capstone Press, 2019.

Troupe, Thomas Kingsley. *Extreme Ghost Stories.* Mankato, Minn.: Black Rabbit Books, 2019.

ON THE WEB

FACTSURFER

Factsurfer.com gives you a safe, fun way to find more information.

1. Go to www.factsurfer.com.

2. Enter "ghosts in Asia" into the search box and click 🔍.

3. Select your book cover to see a list of related content.

INDEX